MAD LIBS
QUICK REVIEW

In case you have forgotten what adjectives, adverbs, nouns, and verbs are, here is a quick review:

An ADJECTIVE describes something or somebody. *Lumpy*, *soft*, *ugly*, *messy*, and *short* are adjectives.

An ADVERB tells how something is done. It modifies a verb and usually ends in "ly." *Modestly*, *stupidly*, *greedily*, and *carefully* are adverbs.

A NOUN is the name of a person, place, or thing. *Sidewalk*, *umbrella*, *bridle*, *bathtub*, and *nose* are nouns.

A VERB is an action word. *Run*, *pitch*, *jump*, and *swim* are verbs. Put the verbs in past tense if the directions say PAST TENSE. *Ran*, *pitched*, *jumped*, and *swam* are verbs in the past tense.

When we ask for A PLACE, we mean any sort of place: a country or city (*Spain*, *Cleveland*) or a room (*bathroom*, *kitchen*).

An EXCLAMATION or SILLY WORD is any sort of funny sound, gasp, grunt, or outcry, like *Wow!*, *Ouch!*, *Whomp!*, *Ick!*, and *Gadzooks!*

When we ask for specific words, like a NUMBER, a COLOR, an ANIMAL, or a PART OF THE BODY, we mean a word that is one of those things, like *seven*, *blue*, *horse*, or *head*.

When we ask for a PLURAL, it means more than one. For example, *cat* pluralized is *cats*.

MAD LIBS® is fun to play with friends, but you can also play it by yourself! To begin with, DO NOT look at the story on the page below. Fill in the blanks on this page with the words called for. Then, using the words you have selected, fill in the blank spaces in the story.

Now you've created your own hilarious MAD LIBS® game!

THE ART OF ESPIONAGE

VERB ENDING IN "ING" _____

ADJECTIVE _____

ADJECTIVE _____

PLURAL NOUN _____

ADJECTIVE _____

PERSON IN ROOM _____

PLURAL NOUN _____

A PLACE _____

ADJECTIVE _____

CELEBRITY _____

NOUN _____

PLURAL NOUN _____

ADJECTIVE _____

PLURAL NOUN _____

PLURAL NOUN _____

NOUN _____

PLURAL NOUN _____

MAD LIBS®

SPY MAD LIBS

concept created by Roger Price & Leonard Stern

PSS!
PRICE STERN SLOAN
An Imprint of Penguin Group (USA) Inc.

PRICE STERN SLOAN
Published by the Penguin Group
Penguin Group (USA) Inc., 375 Hudson Street, New York, New York 10014, USA
Penguin Group (Canada), 90 Eglinton Avenue East, Suite 700,
Toronto, Ontario M4P 2Y3, Canada
(a division of Pearson Penguin Canada Inc.)
Penguin Books Ltd., 80 Strand, London WC2R 0RL, England
Penguin Group Ireland, 25 St. Stephen's Green, Dublin 2, Ireland
(a division of Penguin Books Ltd.)
Penguin Group (Australia), 250 Camberwell Road, Camberwell, Victoria 3124, Australia
(a division of Pearson Australia Group Pty. Ltd.)
Penguin Books India Pvt. Ltd., 11 Community Centre,
Panchsheel Park, New Delhi—110 017, India
Penguin Group (NZ), 67 Apollo Drive, Rosedale, Auckland 0632, New Zealand
(a division of Pearson New Zealand Ltd.)
Penguin Books (South Africa) (Pty.) Ltd., 24 Sturdee Avenue,
Rosebank, Johannesburg 2196, South Africa

Penguin Books Ltd., Registered Offices:
80 Strand, London WC2R 0RL, England

Mad Libs format and text copyright © 2012 by Price Stern Sloan,
an imprint of Penguin Group (USA) Inc.

Published by Price Stern Sloan,
a division of Penguin Young Readers Group,
345 Hudson Street, New York, New York 10014.

ISBN 978-0-8431-7297-3

7 9 10 8

MAD LIBS
INSTRUCTIONS

MAD LIBS® is a game for people who don't like games!
It can be played by one, two, three, four, or forty.

● RIDICULOUSLY SIMPLE DIRECTIONS

In this tablet you will find stories containing blank spaces where words
are left out. One player, the READER, selects one of these stories. The
READER does not tell anyone what the story is about. Instead, he/she asks
the other players, the WRITERS, to give him/her words. These words are
used to fill in the blank spaces in the story.

● TO PLAY

The READER asks each WRITER in turn to call out a word—an adjective or
a noun or whatever the space calls for—and uses them to fill in the blank
spaces in the story. The result is a MAD LIBS® game.

When the READER then reads the completed MAD LIBS® game to the other
players, they will discover that they have written a story that is fantastic,
screamingly funny, shocking, silly, crazy, or just plain dumb—depending
upon which words each WRITER called out.

● EXAMPLE (*Before* and *After*)

"_____!" he said _____
      EXCLAMATION   ADVERB

as he jumped into his convertible _____ and
                                       NOUN

drove off with his _____ wife.
                   ADJECTIVE

"_____*Ouch*_____!" he said _____*stupidly*_____
      EXCLAMATION   ADVERB

as he jumped into his convertible _____*cat*_____ and
                                       NOUN

drove off with his _____*brave*_____ wife.
                   ADJECTIVE

MAD LIBS
THE ART OF ESPIONAGE

Espionage is the formal word for _____. In the

VERB ENDING IN "ING"

shadowy world of spies, a/an _____ organization like the

ADJECTIVE

US government uses spies to infiltrate _____ groups for the

ADJECTIVE

purpose of obtaining top secret _____. For example,

PLURAL NOUN

spies might have to crack the code for accessing confidential,

_____ files, or their mission could be far more dangerous—

ADJECTIVE

like stealing the key ingredient for making _____'s award-

PERSON IN ROOM

winning Explosive Fudgy _____. Spies are found all over

PLURAL NOUN

(the) _____—but they are not allowed to reveal their

A PLACE

_____ identities. A teacher, _____, or even

ADJECTIVE · CELEBRITY

the little old _____ with the cane and fifteen pet

NOUN

_____ who lives next door to you could be a spy. The world

PLURAL NOUN

of spying might seem glamorous and _____—but it's filled

ADJECTIVE

with risks and _____! Sure, spies have a never-ending supply

PLURAL NOUN

of supercool electronic _____, but they can't trust any

PLURAL NOUN

_____—which is why the number one rule of spies is to

NOUN

keep friends close—and _____ closer!

PLURAL NOUN

MAD LIBS® is fun to play with friends, but you can also play it by yourself! To begin with, DO NOT look at the story on the page below. Fill in the blanks on this page with the words called for. Then, using the words you have selected, fill in the blank spaces in the story.

Now you've created your own hilarious MAD LIBS® game!

SPY HALL OF FAME

PLURAL NOUN _____

ADJECTIVE _____

PERSON IN ROOM (MALE) _____

NUMBER _____

ADJECTIVE _____

NOUN _____

PART OF THE BODY _____

ADJECTIVE _____

PART OF THE BODY _____

ADJECTIVE _____

PLURAL NOUN _____

NOUN _____

PART OF THE BODY _____

NOUN _____

NOUN _____

VERB _____

CELEBRITY _____

NOUN _____

MAD LIBS

SPY HALL OF FAME

The Spy Hall of Fame honors the brave _____ of that
PLURAL NOUN

_____ profession known as spying. Inductees include:
ADJECTIVE

• _____ **Bond**—Famously known as Agent Double
PERSON IN ROOM (MALE)

"O" _____, this spy was as handsome as he was _____.
NUMBER   ADJECTIVE

Not only did Bond nab the bad _____ every time, he always
NOUN

won the _____ of the _____ woman as well.
PART OF THE BODY   ADJECTIVE

• **Chuck "Eagle _____" Spyglass**—Whether it was
PART OF THE BODY

designing a/an _____ pair of night-vision _____ or
ADJECTIVE   PLURAL NOUN

hiding a tiny camera inside a gold _____ that a spy could
NOUN

wear around his _____. Chuck was the go-to _____
PART OF THE BODY   NOUN

for his wizardry in surveillance.

• **Joe the Spy**—Joe was your typical _____ next door. His
NOUN

high school yearbook denoted him as "Most Likely to _____."
VERB

Who would have thought this Average Joe would be the _____
CELEBRITY

of the spy world when he single-handedly took down an

international ring of _____ robbers?!
NOUN

MAD LIBS® is fun to play with friends, but you can also play it by yourself! To begin with, DO NOT look at the story on the page below. Fill in the blanks on this page with the words called for. Then, using the words you have selected, fill in the blank spaces in the story.

Now you've created your own hilarious MAD LIBS® game!

HOW TO SPEAK LIKE A SPY

ADJECTIVE _____

NOUN _____

VERB _____

NOUN _____

VERB ENDING IN "ING" _____

PLURAL NOUN _____

ADJECTIVE _____

NOUN _____

ADJECTIVE _____

CELEBRITY _____

PERSON IN ROOM _____

NOUN _____

NOUN _____

PLURAL NOUN _____

ADJECTIVE _____

PLURAL NOUN _____

MAD☺LIBS®
HOW TO SPEAK LIKE A SPY

Spies speak their own _____ language. Common terms include:
ADJECTIVE

• **Target**—a person or a/an _____ of interest whom a spy
NOUN

watches come and _____
VERB

• **Surveillance**—to monitor or observe a/an _____ with
NOUN

visual, listening, or _____ equipment like cameras,
VERB ENDING IN "ING"

satellites, or long-distance _____
PLURAL NOUN

• **Bug**—a/an _____ device that can be planted on an object
ADJECTIVE

such as a car, remote control, or _____ phone to listen in on
NOUN

a target's _____ conversations
ADJECTIVE

• **Alias**—the name a spy uses—like _____ or _____—
CELEBRITY   PERSON IN ROOM

while undercover

• **Mole**—a/an _____ from one spy organization who gets a
NOUN

job within a rival _____ organization in order to obtain
NOUN

inside information or other secret _____
PLURAL NOUN

• **Classified**—sensitive and _____ information that only
ADJECTIVE

certain levels of _____ have authorized clearance to access
PLURAL NOUN

From SPY MAD LIBS® • Copyright © 2012 by Price Stern Sloan,
an imprint of Penguin Group (USA) Inc., 345 Hudson Street, New York, NY 10014.

MAD LIBS® is fun to play with friends, but you can also play it by yourself! To begin with, DO NOT look at the story on the page below. Fill in the blanks on this page with the words called for. Then, using the words you have selected, fill in the blank spaces in the story.

Now you've created your own hilarious MAD LIBS® game!

A SPY BIRTHDAY PARTY

NUMBER _____

NOUN _____

ADJECTIVE _____

PLURAL NOUN _____

ADJECTIVE _____

PART OF THE BODY (PLURAL) _____

ADJECTIVE _____

VERB _____

ADJECTIVE _____

PLURAL NOUN _____

NOUN _____

NOUN _____

PLURAL NOUN _____

PART OF THE BODY (PLURAL) _____

PLURAL NOUN _____

ADJECTIVE _____

ADJECTIVE _____

NOUN _____

PLURAL NOUN _____

MAD LIBS

A SPY BIRTHDAY PARTY

When I turned _____ years old, my mom and _____
NUMBER   NOUN

threw a/an _____ spy-themed birthday party for me. I invited
ADJECTIVE

ten of my closest _____, and we spent a/an _____
PLURAL NOUN   ADJECTIVE

afternoon doing cool spy stuff. We slipped black sunglasses over our

_____, grabbed _____ toy cell phones, and
PART OF THE BODY (PLURAL)   ADJECTIVE

practiced our surveillance techniques with a game of hide-and-

_____ around my backyard. We decoded _____
VERB   ADJECTIVE

messages that my parents had written on colorful _____.
PLURAL NOUN

We pounded on a/an _____-shaped piñata with a wooden
NOUN

_____, and we put spy tattoos like binoculars, computers,
NOUN

and micro-_____ all over our _____. Later
PLURAL NOUN   PART OF THE BODY (PLURAL)

my mom served cake and _____, and everyone sang
PLURAL NOUN

"_____ Birthday" to me. I got a ton of _____ gifts,
ADJECTIVE   ADJECTIVE

but my favorite was the motion-activated _____ that would
NOUN

alert me to any _____ about to sneak into my room. Every
PLURAL NOUN

good spy needs one of these!

MAD LIBS® is fun to play with friends, but you can also play it by yourself! To begin with, DO NOT look at the story on the page below. Fill in the blanks on this page with the words called for. Then, using the words you have selected, fill in the blank spaces in the story.

Now you've created your own hilarious MAD LIBS® game!

FROM THE SPY FILE

PERSON IN ROOM _____

ADJECTIVE _____

CELEBRITY _____

VERB ENDING IN "ING" _____

NOUN _____

ADJECTIVE _____

ADJECTIVE _____

NOUN _____

ADJECTIVE _____

ADJECTIVE _____

A PLACE _____

ADJECTIVE _____

NOUN _____

PART OF THE BODY _____

PLURAL NOUN _____

ADJECTIVE _____

PART OF THE BODY _____

ADJECTIVE _____

MAD LIBS®
FROM THE SPY FILE

To Agent _____: At this morning's _____
      PERSON IN ROOM   ADJECTIVE

management meeting, it was decided by Agency Chief _____
                                                              CELEBRITY

that you are being assigned to the case known internally as

Operation _____ _____. This memo will
         VERB ENDING IN "ING"   NOUN

provide the _____ details of the case, and you will be briefed
            ADJECTIVE

further in the coming week. As you may know, this case involves a

band of _____ thieves who stole the blueprints to a top secret
         ADJECTIVE

robot _____ that threatens the security of our _____
        NOUN   ADJECTIVE

country. They have hidden the prints somewhere in a/an

_____ location on the outskirts of (the) _____.
  ADJECTIVE   A PLACE

Their leader's name is Uno Ojo, which translates to _____
                                                         ADJECTIVE

_____. You will know him by the black eye patch he wears
   NOUN

over his _____. Be advised that he and his group of evil
         PART OF THE BODY

_____ are armed and _____, so use extreme caution
  PLURAL NOUN   ADJECTIVE

if you come face-to-_____ with any of them. As any good spy
                    PART OF THE BODY

knows, you're of no use to the agency if you're _____.
                                                    ADJECTIVE

MAD LIBS® is fun to play with friends, but you can also play it by yourself! To begin with, DO NOT look at the story on the page below. Fill in the blanks on this page with the words called for. Then, using the words you have selected, fill in the blank spaces in the story.

Now you've created your own hilarious MAD LIBS® game!

WELCOME TO HEADQUARTERS

NOUN _____

VERB _____

ADJECTIVE _____

ADJECTIVE _____

NOUN _____

PERSON IN ROOM _____

ADJECTIVE _____

PLURAL NOUN _____

PART OF THE BODY _____

CELEBRITY _____

ADJECTIVE _____

PLURAL NOUN _____

VERB ENDING IN "ING" _____

PART OF THE BODY _____

The new spy headquarters that just opened on the corner of Fifth

Avenue and _____ Street really makes people stop and
             NOUN

_____. The building itself features _____, modern
   VERB   ADJECTIVE

architecture on the outside and _____, state-of-the-
                                   ADJECTIVE

art technology on the inside. To gain entrance, you must step

through an electronic _____ while a security guard named
                         NOUN

_____ pats you down with a/an _____ wand to
PERSON IN ROOM   ADJECTIVE

make sure you aren't carrying any dangerous _____. Then
                                              PLURAL NOUN

you have to wear a name badge around your _____ that
                                            PART OF THE BODY

says, "Hi! My name is _____." There's a/an _____
                         CELEBRITY   ADJECTIVE

elevator to take you anywhere you need to go. There are closed-

circuit _____ everywhere, so if anyone in the building starts
           PLURAL NOUN

_____ inappropriately, security will instantly remove
VERB ENDING IN "ING"

them. Certain areas are completely off-limits—unless, of course,

you place your _____ on the scanner and it gives you
                  PART OF THE BODY

authorized clearance.

MAD LIBS® is fun to play with friends, but you can also play it by yourself! To begin with, DO NOT look at the story on the page below. Fill in the blanks on this page with the words called for. Then, using the words you have selected, fill in the blank spaces in the story.

Now you've created your own hilarious MAD LIBS® game!

GEAR & GADGETS, PART 1

ADJECTIVE _____

ADJECTIVE _____

PART OF THE BODY _____

NOUN _____

PLURAL NOUN _____

PLURAL NOUN _____

ADJECTIVE _____

COLOR _____

VERB ENDING IN "ING" _____

TYPE OF LIQUID _____

ADJECTIVE _____

ADJECTIVE _____

CELEBRITY _____

PART OF THE BODY (PLURAL) _____

VERB ENDING IN "ING" _____

One of the most _____ parts about being a spy are the gadgets
                    ADJECTIVE

you get to use! Here are some examples:

- **Spy phones**—These do much more than make _____ calls.
                                                   ADJECTIVE

  They can scan _____-prints on a drinking _____
                 PART OF THE BODY   NOUN

  or shoot laser _____ if a spy is being chased.
                  PLURAL NOUN

- **X-ray vision** _____—These _____ glasses are so
                    PLURAL NOUN   ADJECTIVE

  powerful that they can help spies determine if an enemy is wearing

  _____ underwear.
   COLOR

- _____ beans—A must-have defense weapon for any
   VERB ENDING IN "ING"

  spy, the beans are dropped in a glass of _____ to render an
                                            TYPE OF LIQUID

  enemy _____.
         ADJECTIVE

- **Mini flashlight**—This clever and _____ little tool projects
                                       ADJECTIVE

  a holographic image of _____ to distract bad guys.
                          CELEBRITY

- **Eavesdropping ears**—Spies affix long-range earpieces to their

  _____ to detect where their targets are
   PART OF THE BODY (PLURAL)

  _____.
   VERB ENDING IN "ING"

MAD LIBS® is fun to play with friends, but you can also play it by yourself! To begin with, DO NOT look at the story on the page below. Fill in the blanks on this page with the words called for. Then, using the words you have selected, fill in the blank spaces in the story.

Now you've created your own hilarious MAD LIBS® game!

I, SPY

PERSON IN ROOM _____

NUMBER _____

ADJECTIVE _____

ADJECTIVE _____

A PLACE _____

NOUN _____

ADJECTIVE _____

PLURAL NOUN _____

SILLY WORD _____

PART OF THE BODY _____

ADJECTIVE _____

CELEBRITY _____

VERB ENDING IN "ING" _____

PLURAL NOUN _____

NOUN _____

PLURAL NOUN _____

ADJECTIVE _____

PLURAL NOUN _____

ADJECTIVE _____

PART OF THE BODY (PLURAL) _____

MAD LIBS®

I, SPY

My name is _____, and I became a spy when I was only
                    PERSON IN ROOM

_____ years old. It certainly was an exciting, _____
        NUMBER   ADJECTIVE

time in my life! I was sent to _____ locations all over the
                                              ADJECTIVE

world, including London, Paris, and (the) _____.
                                                         A PLACE

Depending on the assignment, there could be _____ chases,
                                                               NOUN

_____ explosions, or _____ collapsing around me.
      ADJECTIVE   PLURAL NOUN

_____, I'm lucky I didn't lose a/an _____ during
    SILLY WORD   PART OF THE BODY

some of my _____ spy adventures! One time my partner
                  ADJECTIVE

_____ and I were _____ in an alley in pursuit
    CELEBRITY   VERB ENDING IN "ING"

of a target when a shower of flaming _____ shot out of the
                                                  PLURAL NOUN

darkness. Another time I was piloting a/an _____ when a
                                                        NOUN

flock of _____ flew right into the engines. Fortunately, I
              PLURAL NOUN

crash-landed in a/an _____ lake, so I managed to walk away
                            ADJECTIVE

with only a few scrapes and _____. Now that I'm retired, my
                                      PLURAL NOUN

life isn't nearly as _____, but on the other hand, it's nice just
                          ADJECTIVE

to be able to put my _____ up and relax.
                            PART OF THE BODY (PLURAL)

MAD LIBS® is fun to play with friends, but you can also play it by yourself! To begin with, DO NOT look at the story on the page below. Fill in the blanks on this page with the words called for. Then, using the words you have selected, fill in the blank spaces in the story.

Now you've created your own hilarious MAD LIBS® game!

DRESSING IN DISGUISE

ADJECTIVE _____

ARTICLE OF CLOTHING (PLURAL) _____

ADJECTIVE _____

CELEBRITY _____

PERSON IN ROOM (MALE) _____

ADJECTIVE _____

PART OF THE BODY _____

NOUN _____

PLURAL NOUN _____

VERB _____

PLURAL NOUN _____

ADJECTIVE _____

PLURAL NOUN _____

COLOR _____

ADJECTIVE _____

PART OF THE BODY (PLURAL) _____

MAD LIBS®
DRESSING IN DISGUISE

A superspy must excel in the _____ art of disguise. He
                                      ADJECTIVE

needs to be able to use _____, makeup, and
                            ARTICLE OF CLOTHING (PLURAL)

_____ acting skills to morph into other characters, such
       ADJECTIVE

as a superstar like _____ or just a regular guy like
                          CELEBRITY

_____. Disguises can range from simple to outrageously
PERSON IN ROOM (MALE)

_____. One of the easiest disguises is a pair of eyeglasses with
       ADJECTIVE

a large _____ and mustache attached. Other disguises are
        PART OF THE BODY

more complicated, like a full-body _____ costume. Sometimes
                                        NOUN

male spies even have to dress as female _____—a particularly
                                           PLURAL NOUN

challenging disguise as it's difficult to _____ while wearing a
                                             VERB

dress and high _____! Once a person advances to the level of
                PLURAL NOUN

spy, he's given a/an _____ Spy Disguise Kit containing
                        ADJECTIVE

everything he needs to become anyone he wants. The kits contain

helpful disguise tools like _____ to color your hair
                                PLURAL NOUN

_____, _____ wigs, and—best of all—fake
       COLOR   ADJECTIVE

_____.
PART OF THE BODY (PLURAL)

From SPY MAD LIBS® • Copyright © 2012 by Price Stern Sloan,
an imprint of Penguin Group (USA) Inc., 345 Hudson Street, New York, NY 10014.

MAD LIBS® is fun to play with friends, but you can also play it by yourself! To begin with, DO NOT look at the story on the page below. Fill in the blanks on this page with the words called for. Then, using the words you have selected, fill in the blank spaces in the story.

Now you've created your own hilarious MAD LIBS® game!

ULTIMATE SPY MOBILE

NOUN _____

ADJECTIVE _____

PLURAL NOUN _____

NOUN _____

SILLY WORD _____

PLURAL NOUN _____

VERB _____

ADJECTIVE _____

NOUN _____

PART OF THE BODY _____

PLURAL NOUN _____

PLURAL NOUN _____

ADJECTIVE _____

NOUN _____

NOUN _____

ADJECTIVE _____

CELEBRITY _____

MAD LIBS®
ULTIMATE SPY MOBILE

A top-notch spy deserves to drive a world-class _____ with all
                                                      NOUN

these _____ features:
         ADJECTIVE

- Computers and TV monitors to communicate with _____
                                                      PLURAL NOUN

  back at headquarters

- _____-activated doors that slide open when the password
     NOUN

  "_____" is spoken
     SILLY WORD

- Jet sprays that shoot _____ so that any enemy in pursuit
                            PLURAL NOUN

  will crash and _____
                     VERB

- A/an _____ punching _____ that will bonk an
           ADJECTIVE   NOUN

  enemy on the _____ if he gets inside the vehicle
                  PART OF THE BODY

- Razor-sharp _____ along the outside edges of the car to
                  PLURAL NOUN

  slice the tires of other passing _____
                                      PLURAL NOUN

- A/an _____ battering ram on the front end to bash into
           ADJECTIVE

  a/an _____ barricade
          NOUN

- _____-boosters that will propel the vehicle into the air
     NOUN

- Best of all, a/an _____ sound system that fills the vehicle
                       ADJECTIVE

  with the sweet melodies of _____
                                CELEBRITY

From SPY MAD LIBS® • Copyright © 2012 by Price Stern Sloan,
an imprint of Penguin Group (USA) Inc., 345 Hudson Street, New York, NY 10014.

MAD LIBS® is fun to play with friends, but you can also play it by yourself! To begin with, DO NOT look at the story on the page below. Fill in the blanks on this page with the words called for. Then, using the words you have selected, fill in the blank spaces in the story.

Now you've created your own hilarious MAD LIBS® game!

A TRIP TO
THE SPY MUSEUM

A PLACE _____

ADJECTIVE _____

VERB ENDING IN "ING" _____

PLURAL NOUN _____

PLURAL NOUN _____

ADJECTIVE _____

NOUN _____

PLURAL NOUN _____

ADJECTIVE _____

VERB ENDING IN "ING" _____

PLURAL NOUN _____

NOUN _____

ADJECTIVE _____

VERB ENDING IN "ING" _____

NOUN _____

ADJECTIVE _____

NOUN _____

PLURAL NOUN _____

ADJECTIVE _____

MAD LIBS

A TRIP TO THE SPY MUSEUM

Located in (the) _____, the International Spy Museum is the
           A PLACE

only _____ museum in the United States dedicated to
     ADJECTIVE

the covert profession of _____. The museum features the
            VERB ENDING IN "ING"

largest collection of spy-themed _____ ever placed on public
           PLURAL NOUN

display. These items bring to life the work of famous _____
           PLURAL NOUN

as well as history-making _____ espionage missions. The
        ADJECTIVE

stories of spies are told through films, an interactive _____,
           NOUN

and state-of-the-art _____. The museum contains a/an
       PLURAL NOUN

_____ gift shop and a restaurant called _____
  ADJECTIVE   VERB ENDING IN "ING"

Spy Café. Young _____ love to visit the spy museum for
        PLURAL NOUN

_____ parties, field trips, and _____ scavenger
  NOUN   ADJECTIVE

hunts. The exhibits teach up-and-_____ spies about
              VERB ENDING IN "ING"

_____ surveillance, threat analysis, and maintaining one's
  NOUN

_____ cover. The goal of the International _____
  ADJECTIVE   NOUN

Museum is to teach _____ about espionage in a fun,
        PLURAL NOUN

_____ way. Who knows? It might make them want to join
  ADJECTIVE

the team someday!

MAD LIBS® is fun to play with friends, but you can also play it by yourself! To begin with, DO NOT look at the story on the page below. Fill in the blanks on this page with the words called for. Then, using the words you have selected, fill in the blank spaces in the story.

Now you've created your own hilarious MAD LIBS® game!

THE BEST SPY MOVIES

NOUN _____

ADVERB _____

PLURAL NOUN _____

NOUN _____

PERSON IN ROOM (MALE) _____

ADJECTIVE _____

CELEBRITY _____

NOUN _____

ADJECTIVE _____

PERSON IN ROOM (FEMALE) _____

NOUN _____

NOUN _____

NOUN _____

PART OF THE BODY _____

ADJECTIVE _____

COLOR _____

PART OF THE BODY _____

TYPE OF FOOD _____

MAD LIBS

THE BEST SPY MOVIES

Here are the best spy movies to curl up on the _____
NOUN

and watch:

- *Spy Story*: In this _____ colorful tale, toy _____
  ADVERB   PLURAL NOUN

  come to life! The main character is a space-_____ named
                                                  NOUN

  _____ Lightyear who thinks he is an intergalactic
  PERSON IN ROOM (MALE)

  spy, and a/an _____ cowboy action figure named
                  ADJECTIVE

  _____ must convince him he's just a/an _____.
  CELEBRITY   NOUN

- *Beauty and the Spy*: A beautiful, _____ young girl named
                                        ADJECTIVE

  _____ wanders into a castle in the middle of
  PERSON IN ROOM (FEMALE)

  a/an _____ and meets a spy who's under the spell of a
         NOUN

  wicked, old _____. He has been turned into a hideous
                NOUN

  _____ with hair all over his _____ and only she
  NOUN   PART OF THE BODY

  can break the enchantment.

- *Spy Wars*: A space tale in which spies from the _____ Rebel
                                                      ADJECTIVE

  Forces go up against a scary, robotic man in flowing _____
                                                          COLOR

  robes who wears a large helmet on his _____ and calls
                                            PART OF THE BODY

  himself Lord _____.
                TYPE OF FOOD

From SPY MAD LIBS® • Copyright © 2012 by Price Stern Sloan,
an imprint of Penguin Group (USA) Inc., 345 Hudson Street, New York, NY 10014.

MAD LIBS® is fun to play with friends, but you can also play it by yourself! To begin with, DO NOT look at the story on the page below. Fill in the blanks on this page with the words called for. Then, using the words you have selected, fill in the blank spaces in the story.

Now you've created your own hilarious MAD LIBS® game!

TALES FROM SPY CAMP

ADJECTIVE _____

NOUN _____

VERB _____

ADJECTIVE _____

CELEBRITY _____

PLURAL NOUN _____

PLURAL NOUN _____

ADJECTIVE _____

VERB _____

PLURAL NOUN _____

ADVERB _____

EXCLAMATION _____

NOUN _____

PART OF THE BODY _____

VERB _____

NOUN _____

PLURAL NOUN _____

PLURAL NOUN _____

PERSON IN ROOM _____

MAD LIBS

TALES FROM SPY CAMP

Dear Mom and Dad,

Spy Camp is totally _____! Being a real _____-
                         ADJECTIVE   NOUN
in-training is the coolest thing ever! We start each day with a

_____ around the campground for exercise. Next we do
        VERB

different _____ activities that Counselor _____
              ADJECTIVE   CELEBRITY

assigns. Sometimes we get buckets full of screws, magnets, and other

_____ to build surveillance gadgets. Or we use leaves, twigs,
   PLURAL NOUN

and _____ to make camouflage disguises. My favorite is
        PLURAL NOUN

when we play _____ games like Spy Paintball. We team up
                   ADJECTIVE

and _____ behind trees, boulders, and other large
           VERB

_____. We need to be _____ stealthy to avoid
   PLURAL NOUN   ADVERB

detection; otherwise, we'll get nailed—and, _____, a
                                                      EXCLAMATION

paintball _____ to the _____ really hurts! Sometimes
                NOUN   PART OF THE BODY

we just _____ by a roaring _____ and roast
               VERB   NOUN

_____—like regular campers do. See you in a few weeks!
   PLURAL NOUN

Hugs and _____, _____
              PLURAL NOUN   PERSON IN ROOM

MAD LIBS® is fun to play with friends, but you can also play it by yourself! To begin with, DO NOT look at the story on the page below. Fill in the blanks on this page with the words called for. Then, using the words you have selected, fill in the blank spaces in the story.

Now you've created your own hilarious MAD LIBS® game!

WANTED:
A FEW GOOD SPIES

ADJECTIVE _____

PART OF THE BODY (PLURAL) _____

NOUN _____

TYPE OF FOOD _____

ADJECTIVE _____

A PLACE _____

ADJECTIVE _____

ADJECTIVE _____

PART OF THE BODY (PLURAL) _____

ADJECTIVE _____

ADJECTIVE _____

ARTICLE OF CLOTHING (PLURAL) _____

NUMBER _____

PLURAL NOUN _____

NOUN _____

VERB _____

MAD LIBS®
WANTED:
A FEW GOOD SPIES

Are you sneaky and _____? Do you keep your eyes and
                          ADJECTIVE

_____ open at all times to things going on around
PART OF THE BODY (PLURAL)

you? Can you take items like a piece of string, a cell phone, a/an

_____, and some day-old _____ and build a
      NOUN   TYPE OF FOOD

makeshift homing device to track a/an _____ target? If so,
                                          ADJECTIVE

then we want you to join our exclusive spy agency. We are hired out by

the military, private corporations, and occasionally the mayor of (the)

_____ to infiltrate a/an _____ enemy and steal
     A PLACE   ADJECTIVE

plans, crack codes, or perform other _____ duties as assigned.
                                          ADJECTIVE

Although previous experience is not required, candidates who are

fast on their _____ when it comes to solving
                PART OF THE BODY (PLURAL)

_____ problems will be given top consideration. Spy
      ADJECTIVE

gear—including a backpack of _____ gadgets and black
                                  ADJECTIVE

_____—is provided. Starting salary is _____
ARTICLE OF CLOTHING (PLURAL)   NUMBER

_____ a week. If you can move with the stealth of a two-ton
   PLURAL NOUN

_____, then the job of a spy could be right for you.
     NOUN

_____ today for an application!
     VERB

From SPY MAD LIBS® • Copyright © 2012 by Price Stern Sloan,
an imprint of Penguin Group (USA) Inc., 345 Hudson Street, New York, NY 10014.

MAD LIBS® is fun to play with friends, but you can also play it by yourself! To begin with, DO NOT look at the story on the page below. Fill in the blanks on this page with the words called for. Then, using the words you have selected, fill in the blank spaces in the story.

Now you've created your own hilarious MAD LIBS® game!

ODE TO SPIES

VERB ENDING IN "ING" _____

NOUN _____

ADJECTIVE _____

PLURAL NOUN _____

PLURAL NOUN _____

VERB _____

PART OF THE BODY (PLURAL) _____

ADJECTIVE _____

NOUN _____

NOUN _____

VERB _____

ADJECTIVE _____

PLURAL NOUN _____

PLURAL NOUN _____

PERSON IN ROOM _____

ADJECTIVE _____

NOUN _____

MAD LIBS

ODE TO SPIES

They're pros at _____ stealthily and the art of surprise.
　　　　　　　　VERB ENDING IN "ING"

Is that a/an _____ that I see—or a/an _____ spy
　　　　　　　NOUN　　　　　　　　　　　　　　　ADJECTIVE

in disguise?

They're sneaky as _____ so their covers don't get blown.
　　　　　　　　　PLURAL NOUN

They hang with their best _____, but they *always*
　　　　　　　　　　　　　　PLURAL NOUN

_____ alone.
　VERB

Spies think with their _____, and they're fast on
　　　　　　　　　　　PART OF THE BODY (PLURAL)

their feet.

The high-tech gadgets they use are _____ and neat,
　　　　　　　　　　　　　　　　ADJECTIVE

Like _____-shaped bugs to plant on a moving car
　　　NOUN

Or telescopic _____-glasses to help them _____ far.
　　　　　　　NOUN　　　　　　　　　　　　　VERB

They crack _____ codes with _____ and speed.
　　　　　ADJECTIVE　　　　　　PLURAL NOUN

Steal _____? Learn secrets? They'll get what you need!
　　　PLURAL NOUN

So don't you fear, _____ ! Don't make a/an
　　　　　　　　　PERSON IN ROOM

_____ fuss!
　ADJECTIVE

Just pick up the _____ and dial 1-800-SPIES-R-US.
　　　　　　　　NOUN

MAD LIBS® is fun to play with friends, but you can also play it by yourself! To begin with, DO NOT look at the story on the page below. Fill in the blanks on this page with the words called for. Then, using the words you have selected, fill in the blank spaces in the story.

Now you've created your own hilarious MAD LIBS® game!

MOST WANTED LIST

PLURAL NOUN _____

ADJECTIVE _____

PLURAL NOUN _____

NOUN _____

ADVERB _____

NOUN _____

ADJECTIVE _____

PERSON IN ROOM _____

COLOR _____

NOUN _____

PART OF THE BODY (PLURAL) _____

PLURAL NOUN _____

NOUN _____

A PLACE _____

CELEBRITY _____

NOUN _____

ADJECTIVE _____

PLURAL NOUN _____

PART OF THE BODY (PLURAL) _____

PLURAL NOUN _____

MAD LIBS

MOST WANTED LIST

The Global Spy Organization's list of most wanted _____
                                                    PLURAL NOUN

is a long one. Here are _____ profiles of the most
                          ADJECTIVE

notorious criminals:

- **Max Von** _____ **III** is wanted for the kidnapping of Sir
                PLURAL NOUN

  Puffy-_____, the _____ overweight pet _____
           NOUN   ADVERB   NOUN

  of His _____ Majesty, King _____.
           ADJECTIVE   PERSON IN ROOM

- **The** _____ **Shadow** is the head of an international ring of
            COLOR

  _____ thieves whose sticky _____ have lifted
     NOUN   PART OF THE BODY (PLURAL)

  valuable _____ from museums around the world, including
             PLURAL NOUN

  the famous Le _____ located in (the) _____.
                  NOUN   A PLACE

- _____, a world-famous super-_____, is actually
    CELEBRITY   NOUN

  the mastermind behind a/an _____ group of computer
                               ADJECTIVE

  geeks and techno-_____ whose ultra-intelligent
                     PLURAL NOUN

  _____ enable them to breach the highest levels of
  PART OF THE BODY (PLURAL)

  security and steal US military _____.
                                   PLURAL NOUN

From SPY MAD LIBS® • Copyright © 2012 by Price Stern Sloan,
an imprint of Penguin Group (USA) Inc., 345 Hudson Street, New York, NY 10014.

MAD LIBS® is fun to play with friends, but you can also play it by yourself! To begin with, DO NOT look at the story on the page below. Fill in the blanks on this page with the words called for. Then, using the words you have selected, fill in the blank spaces in the story.

Now you've created your own hilarious MAD LIBS® game!

SPY VIDEO GAMES

PART OF THE BODY (PLURAL) _____

ADJECTIVE _____

COLOR _____

PLURAL NOUN _____

ADJECTIVE _____

A PLACE _____

PLURAL NOUN _____

NOUN _____

PERSON IN ROOM _____

ADJECTIVE _____

PLURAL NOUN _____

NOUN _____

PLURAL NOUN _____

PLURAL NOUN _____

VERB ENDING IN "ING" _____

ADJECTIVE _____

NOUN _____

NUMBER _____

PLURAL NOUN _____

PLURAL NOUN _____

NOUN _____

MAD LIBS®

SPY VIDEO GAMES

Grab your favorite controller, flex your _____, and
PART OF THE BODY (PLURAL)

get ready to play spy in these _____ video games:
ADJECTIVE

• *Operation* _____ _____: You are a spy in the hot,
COLOR _PLURAL NOUN_

_____ jungles of (the) _____. Your mission? Vaporize
ADJECTIVE _A PLACE_

poisonous _____ as you search for the missing and priceless
PLURAL NOUN

_____ Diamond, stolen by the rogue operative,
NOUN

_____.
PERSON IN ROOM

• *Spies in Space*: The _____, evil scientist, Dr. Smarty
ADJECTIVE

_____, has launched a/an _____ into space
PLURAL NOUN _NOUN_

containing deadly _____ that, if sprinkled into the Earth's
PLURAL NOUN

atmosphere, will destroy all living _____.
PLURAL NOUN

• *Speedway Spies*: It's spy-on-spy _____ action on the
VERB ENDING IN "ING"

racetrack! You and your _____ opponent burn up the race
ADJECTIVE

_____ at speeds topping _____ mph as you swerve
NOUN _NUMBER_

to avoid toppling _____, slippery spills of _____,
PLURAL NOUN _PLURAL NOUN_

and, occasionally, a/an _____ trying to cross the road.
NOUN

MAD LIBS® is fun to play with friends, but you can also play it by yourself! To begin with, DO NOT look at the story on the page below. Fill in the blanks on this page with the words called for. Then, using the words you have selected, fill in the blank spaces in the story.

Now you've created your own hilarious MAD LIBS® game!

GEAR & GADGETS, PART 2

ADJECTIVE _____

PLURAL NOUN _____

PLURAL NOUN _____

PLURAL NOUN _____

ADJECTIVE _____

PART OF THE BODY (PLURAL) _____

VERB _____

TYPE OF LIQUID _____

ADJECTIVE _____

PLURAL NOUN _____

VERB _____

PART OF THE BODY (PLURAL) _____

NOUN _____

NOUN _____

PLURAL NOUN _____

PART OF THE BODY (PLURAL) _____

Whether it's to locate a/an _____ target or protect themselves
ADJECTIVE

from enemy _____, spies are always armed with the coolest
PLURAL NOUN

gear and _____ imaginable.
PLURAL NOUN

- **Smoke** _____—When thrown at enemies, these explode
  PLURAL NOUN

  and send _____ smoke billowing into the bad guys'
  ADJECTIVE

  _____, making them unable to _____
  PART OF THE BODY (PLURAL)   VERB

  any longer.

- **Laser Pen**—This tool functions as a pen that writes with invisible

  _____, a telescope so spies can track _____
  TYPE OF LIQUID   ADJECTIVE

  enemies from a safe distance, and a flashlight that contains different

  color _____—yellow means "_____ with caution,"
  PLURAL NOUN   VERB

  blue means "put up your _____ or else," and red
  PART OF THE BODY (PLURAL)

  means "abort the _____."
  NOUN

- **Laser Trip-wire** _____—This gadget has invisible beams
  NOUN

  that alert spies to intruding _____ whenever their
  PLURAL NOUN

  _____ hit the beam.
  PART OF THE BODY (PLURAL)

MAD LIBS® is fun to play with friends, but you can also play it by yourself! To begin with, DO NOT look at the story on the page below. Fill in the blanks on this page with the words called for. Then, using the words you have selected, fill in the blank spaces in the story.

Now you've created your own hilarious MAD LIBS® game!

SPY ROLES

ADJECTIVE _____

NOUN _____

NUMBER _____

PLURAL NOUN _____

PLURAL NOUN _____

NOUN _____

ADJECTIVE _____

NOUN _____

ADJECTIVE _____

PLURAL NOUN _____

ADJECTIVE _____

PLURAL NOUN _____

NOUN _____

PLURAL NOUN _____

ADJECTIVE _____

MAD LIBS

SPY ROLES

There are lots of ways that spies can use their _____ training,
ADJECTIVE

including these:

- A *double agent* is a/an _____ who works for at least
NOUN

_____ intelligence agencies and whose job is to secure
NUMBER

classified _____ at one agency and deliver them to the
PLURAL NOUN

_____ in charge at the other agency.
PLURAL NOUN

- A *sleeper agent* lives as a regular _____ in a foreign country
NOUN

and is only called upon when a hostile or otherwise _____
ADJECTIVE

situation develops.

- A *cobbler* is a/an _____ who creates false passports, diplomas,
NOUN

and other _____ documents to help create identities for
ADJECTIVE

_____ going undercover.
PLURAL NOUN

- A *ghoul* is an agent who searches _____ death notices and
ADJECTIVE

graveyards for names of dead _____ and gives them to
PLURAL NOUN

cobblers for their documents.

- A *handler* is a/an _____ who handles _____ as they
NOUN   PLURAL NOUN

undergo _____ missions.
ADJECTIVE

From SPY MAD LIBS® • Copyright © 2012 by Price Stern Sloan,
an imprint of Penguin Group (USA) Inc., 345 Hudson Street, New York, NY 10014.

MAD LIBS® is fun to play with friends, but you can also play it by yourself! To begin with, DO NOT look at the story on the page below. Fill in the blanks on this page with the words called for. Then, using the words you have selected, fill in the blank spaces in the story.

Now you've created your own hilarious MAD LIBS® game!

SPY U

NOUN _____

ADJECTIVE _____

PLURAL NOUN _____

VERB ENDING IN "ING" _____

PLURAL NOUN _____

CELEBRITY _____

ADJECTIVE _____

ADJECTIVE _____

ADJECTIVE _____

PLURAL NOUN _____

VERB ENDING IN "ING" _____

PERSON IN ROOM _____

A PLACE _____

ADJECTIVE _____

PART OF THE BODY (PLURAL) _____

PLURAL NOUN _____

PART OF THE BODY _____

VERB _____

MAD LIBS

SPY U

Grab a pen and a/an ____________ (NOUN) and get ready to take notes! Spy University offers ____________ (ADJECTIVE) classes for aspiring ____________ (PLURAL NOUN) who wish to enter the covert world of espionage:

- **Introduction to ____________ (VERB ENDING IN "ING"):** Do you have the patience, street smarts, and ____________ (PLURAL NOUN) to be a spy? Taught by world-renowned instructor ____________ (CELEBRITY), this class offers a/an ____________ (ADJECTIVE) overview on what it takes to be a/an ____________ (ADJECTIVE) spy.
- **Stealth Mode:** A great spy has the ____________ (ADJECTIVE) ability to sneak up on unsuspecting ____________ (PLURAL NOUN) without detection. This course provides field experience in ____________ (VERB ENDING IN "ING") within different environments, such as ____________ (PERSON IN ROOM)'s room or even (the) ____________ (A PLACE).
- **Wise Spies:** Spies have many gadgets and ____________ (ADJECTIVE) tools they use to pull the wool over their opponents' ____________ (PART OF THE BODY (PLURAL)). But it's their wits and clever ____________ (PLURAL NOUN) that give them an advantage. Learn how to use your ____________ (PART OF THE BODY) to get your opponent to ____________ (VERB) exactly the way you want him to.

MAD LIBS® is fun to play with friends, but you can also play it by yourself! To begin with, DO NOT look at the story on the page below. Fill in the blanks on this page with the words called for. Then, using the words you have selected, fill in the blank spaces in the story.

Now you've created your own hilarious MAD LIBS® game!

CRACK THE CODE

ADJECTIVE _____

A PLACE _____

ADJECTIVE _____

COLOR _____

VERB ENDING IN "ING" _____

NOUN _____

PART OF THE BODY _____

PLURAL NOUN _____

PLURAL NOUN _____

SAME PLURAL NOUN _____

NOUN _____

ADJECTIVE _____

ADJECTIVE _____

PERSON IN ROOM _____

PLURAL NOUN _____

NOUN _____

A PLACE _____

ADJECTIVE _____

CELEBRITY _____

MAD LIBS
CRACK THE CODE

Cracking _____ codes is a prized spy skill, like in this example:
ADJECTIVE

Coded message: The circus has come to (the) _____, and
A PLACE

there are _____ clowns with big _____ noses
ADJECTIVE   COLOR

_____ in the streets. If you try to run away, they will
VERB ENDING IN "ING"

stick out their _____ and trip you so you fall _____-
NOUN   PART OF THE BODY

first into a puddle of _____. Beware those _____—
PLURAL NOUN   PLURAL NOUN

I repeat, beware those _____!
SAME PLURAL NOUN

Decoded message: To the brave _____ who deciphers this
NOUN

_____ note—be forewarned! Our agency has experienced a
ADJECTIVE

breach of security involving _____ double agents. Agency Chief
ADJECTIVE

_____ desperately needs _____ who have not been
PERSON IN ROOM   PLURAL NOUN

corrupted to be trained as new agents. Report promptly to _____
NOUN

Headquarters located near (the) _____ and await further
A PLACE

instructions. Keep this _____ message confidential. Apply in
ADJECTIVE

person using the code phrase "I am president of the _____
CELEBRITY

Fan Club."

From SPY MAD LIBS® • Copyright © 2012 by Price Stern Sloan,
an imprint of Penguin Group (USA) Inc., 345 Hudson Street, New York, NY 10014.

This book is published by

PSS!

PRICE STERN SLOAN

whose other splendid titles include
such literary classics as

Ad Lib Mad Libs®

Best of Mad Libs®

Camp Daze Mad Libs®

Christmas Carol Mad Libs®

Christmas Fun Mad Libs®

Cool Mad Libs®

Dance Mania Mad Libs®

Dear Valentine Letters Mad Libs®

Dinosaur Mad Libs®

Diva Girl Mad Libs®

Dude, Where's My Mad Libs®

Family Tree Mad Libs®

Fun in the Sun Mad Libs®

Girls Just Wanna Have Mad Libs®

Goofy Mad Libs®

Grab Bag Mad Libs®

Graduation Mad Libs®

Grand Slam Mad Libs®

Hanukkah Mad Libs®

Happily Ever Mad Libs®

Happy Birthday Mad Libs®

Haunted Mad Libs®

Holly, Jolly Mad Libs®

Hot off the Presses Mad Libs®

Kid Libs Mad Libs®

Letters from Camp Mad Libs®

Letters to Mom & Dad Mad Libs®

Mad About Animals Mad Libs®

Mad Libs® for President

Mad Libs® from Outer Space

Mad Libs® in Love

Mad Libs® on the Road

Mad Mad Mad Mad Mad Libs®

Monster Mad Libs®

More Best of Mad Libs®

Night of the Living Mad Libs®

Ninjas Mad Libs®

Off-the-Wall Mad Libs®

The Original #1 Mad Libs®

P. S. I Love Mad Libs®

Peace, Love, and Mad Libs®

Pirates Mad Libs®

Prime-Time Mad Libs®

Rock 'n' Roll Mad Libs®

Slam Dunk Mad Libs®

Sleepover Party Mad Libs®

Son of Mad Libs®

Sooper Dooper Mad Libs®

Spooky Mad Libs®

Straight "A" Mad Libs®

Totally Pink Mad Libs®

Undead Mad Libs®

Upside Down Mad Libs®

Vacation Fun Mad Libs®

We Wish You a Merry Mad Libs®

Winter Games Mad Libs®

You've Got Mad Libs®

and many, many more!
Mad Libs® are available wherever books are sold.